Silenced

A Collection of Poems

By Antanay Tarrant

For years I couldn't make sense of my life, my thoughts, my feelings, or who I was. The feeling of being alone even in a room surrounded by people I loved. Never feeling heard or understood so eventually I stopped talking, until writing became my safe haven from 2014 to this very day.

The more I wrote the more I understood that I wasn't alone, but not everyone was exposing this side of themselves for the fear of being judged. We all feel at some point in time we are being actively judged by family, friends, colleagues, and peers. So as an outcome the random thoughts just stay trapped.

Now those thoughts, my thoughts, are being revealed in the rawest form, directly from my journal. I've been doing the healing in order to share these words with love. There's joy and peace on the other side of pain and I've been protected for this very moment.

To anyone who feels silenced, lost, or alone I hope these poems give you comfort and hope. Healing is always possible as long as you put in the work. I encourage everyone to not only speak your truth but to speak with love. Your words may provide the healing and guidance that your family or friends need.

This is for the outcasts, this is for the black sheep, the shunned, the lost, the unheard, the unseen, the shy, the ones that cry, but most importantly for the ones that still Believe.

Thank you to everyone for the support and love that you've given. I may not know it all, but I do know that our reality is what we make it and there's no victory without a test.

Thank you and Happy Heavenly Birthday to my Papa, this is for you, the protector we can't see. Our glue may be gone but we'll forever stick together with love.

08/08/1958 - 02/23/1999

Read with your eyes,

Listen with your heart

Everything I've been taught is a lie. My entire 24 years of living has been a lie.

A beautiful well thought out lie nonetheless. Everything I thought mattered doesn't.

Everyone I thought genuinely had my best interest never did.

And everything I've been taught is now tainted.

None of it makes sense or aligns with me today and those who THINK they know me won't understand.

Or at least they choose not to understand because they've been conditioned and trapped in their state of mind for decades.

The one thing that has shown to be true is that I'm different.

Different in a good way. Different in a unique way.

Different than everything that I was taught and than everyone that taught it.

Good news is I'm the difference that is shaking the table, telling all truths,

and shedding the light on everything that was once hidden in the shadows.

-Lies and Differences

I stopped writing. I lost myself. I lost my motivation.

I sunk into the place I remember that made me sad, and that is all because...

I stopped writing!

Every day I would say I'm going to start writing again, but never found the strength to pick up that pen.

Not sure if I should be apologizing to myself or those around me, because ever since I stopped writing

I've been trying to find me in everything and everyone else but the man above me...

I stopped writing.

No more excuses, no more waiting, I'm back to it.

My thoughts overflow with unspoken words every day that I cannot express to anyone

or any social media because they are for me and no one else.

Trapped in a world inside my own head not looking for a way out because I'm comfortable.

It's just me and no one else, no disturbances.

Just silence featuring a million thoughts.

I'm not a writer I'm a storyteller. Telling my story but from different perspectives.

Still learning myself at the age of 23, like what do I want to do and who do I want to be.

Only answers I know are that I want to help people

as well as making money so no one has to struggle.

I'm young but my mind is the age of a legend. The wisdom I carry you would think I was older.

I'm more of a listen then speak, observe and peep. Deep down hoping nobody's judging me, but why do I care?

Truth is I don't but I'm a people pleaser, making sure everyone's happy despite my own feelings.

Keep looking for hobbies deciding what I love, truth is

it's right in front of me because it's my own words.

So maybe that's my gift that I refuse to accept and acknowledge.

Maybe that's why I keep looking to arts and crafts when the real magic comes from what's written with this pen.

So who am I? What will I be? I'll be the voice to change a million lives one day, you'll see.

Lost souls walking this Earth looking in everyone else to see a reflection of themselves.

Eyes peeled wide open looking for answers like a child looks for his mother.

You look down you see what you're supposed to be, but look up and see the opposite.

Who's to say which is right and which is wrong, when no one knows the answer.

She feels she's a masculine stud, you tell her she's a feminine princess who needs to learn to be delicate.

You tell him to toughen up and be a man as
he yells at the top of his lungs he just wants to be
held yet nobody hears him.

These lost souls just want to be found, but
maybe they're not really lost they're just
ignored.

She looks at him and sees herself, he looks at her
and sees everything he feels to be his truth.

One day the world will stop, the last penny will
drop, and the rules will no longer exist.

Make sure you've lived for you, that's the one
person you'll be left with.

-Identity

Who broke you like the glass mirror you broke this morning?

Can't stand the sight of yourself because someone told you that you were ugly.

You're looking for love, go stand in the mirror until you find it.

-Self

It's not the same anymore. I don't love you as I once did, and I've tried to force myself to, but I cannot.

The arguing, the back and forth, I am constantly annoyed and triggered. We are not the same anymore

and I know it is time to move on, and I don't know why I stay to try.

You're more like a parent than anything and it upsets me.

STOP THE QUESTIONING!

Let me live my life I am grown, constant battle in my head whether to stay or let go.

You're not who you once were, only person you look out for is yourself, which means I can no longer look out for you.

You've done enough damage to my life, and I cannot allow it anymore.

I have to take back control of my life without you.

As you creep around and do you, I hope you realize all that you do.

You're the one that loved me, but also loved to bring me down.

You're the one that loved me while also loving to point out my flaws and wrongs.

You're the one that loved me, while also loving everyone around me.

That's why we can never be. Things will never be the same.

You're the one that loved painting me as the bad person, and as I know love is not perfect, but love does not live here anymore.

I used to love you

I no longer matter that's fine; I am not a priority
I've accepted it,

I'm someone you keep around to use and you
can't do that anymore.

I'm broken hearted, I'm lonely, I'm lost, I'm hurt,
I'm angry.

I'm all of these bottled-up emotions I can't seem
to express, and that's because of you

but also, some of the blame is on me.

I used to think I knew what love was but not anymore,

now all I can feel is pain and hurt and eventually how to build myself back up.

So, thank you for nothing, thank you for everything,

thank you for giving me wounds and being the one that never worked out.

Now I have the chance to get stronger.

You're not sorry, you never mean a word you say,
but that's fine

because soon enough that will not be my problem.

The day I fully forgive you it will not be because you deserve it because you don't!

it's for me and my freedom and peace of mind.

Not many people have this, not many people want it, depends on what side of the spectrum you grew up on.

It's a love and hate relationship since every personality is so strong.

It'll love you, cherish you, and provide for you every moment.

Or break you down, cause a fuss, make you just want to give up. You don't pick em but you learn to love em.

Everyone has had one, but not all last, so cherish the one you are blessed to have.

-Family

The love of my life came in many forms... or so I thought.

I dreamt up my ideas of love based on what I was taught.

You give and give regardless of how much you can take.

But what if one day I break? Because I thought the love I was being given was what I deserved.

I don't have to be your ride or die, I don't have to take your shit.

But you gone have to show respect because I give the best that I can give.

Who am I? I'm a woman in a generation full of people who just don't get it.

My love is worth more than the disrespect I've been given!

-Fed up

You're the smartest dummy I know. That's what someone close to me told me.

Better yet that's what someone who says they love me told me.

I'm perceived as only being book smart but little do they know

the things in my mind can't be taught from a book or the streets.

I'm observant, tactful, quick on my toes, intelligent, bold, and far from a dummy.

It used to bother me to know that someone who uses the love word could put me down and insult me in many ways.

Until one day I realized it's not me, I can't take it personal they may actually feel that way about themselves.

You can't tell me who I am because I just may be everything you're not.

So, I say in the humblest way, you don't know me and at this rate never will.

-Deflection.

My parents always told me that I'm selfish. Every time I was selfish it's because I did something

FOR ME!!

I can't tell anyone "NO" I can't put my foot down. I'd rather say yes and cry about it later.

My parents always told me because they raised me that I basically owe them.

I have to do what ever they want and be who they want me to be

to keep them happy all because they raised me.

Now I feel that if anyone does anything for me I have to always do what they want me to do.

I don't know how to say No.

I will no longer remain trapped in this system meant to make me small.

A parent can choose to protect or neglect,

stay or leave,

love or hate,

and the child is left with the scars of a lifetime.

You’re too young, you’re misguided, you’ll never understand…

Truth is I understand it all,

but you’re too closed minded to accept what’s presented to you at hand.

-It’s you not me

You apologize like a broken record,

heard it one too many times.

Maybe one day I'll forgive you or....

find the peace in goodbye.

Your words will never define me because

I'm grounded and confident in who I am.

Every hurtful word you throw is a reflection of your soul.

Maybe you should re-evaluate yourself

before you throw anymore stones.

You talk as if you have nothing to lose, you must not know the value of life.

Everything you have can be stripped away, yet you talk as if you're above me.

Who handed you a crown and called you God?

That pedestal is too high for someone who walks the same earth everyday as me.

Who told you that you were superior because of your skin tone?

You must've forgot we all end the same way, in a grave or in ashes.

Souls left to travel with the wind, and probably end up being best friends.

At the gates of heaven what you physically possessed no longer matters, but who you are as a person does.

So step out of that big house, away from everything fancy,

climb off of that high horse and get to know someone outside of you.

-Reality

We're identical yet different,

made with the same things,

but covered with different layers.

We could be great if we just knew how identical we were.

Communication on the surface is an exchange of words,

but go deeper it's the exchange of souls and wisdom.

Tell me about you and I'll tell you about me, maybe even agree to disagree.

Tell me the truth, speak to me your soul, things no one else knows,

because you are too afraid to open up and expose your bare soul.

Speak more life into my heart, but make sure the words are kind,

I'm fragile so give my soul some time to accept what you have to offer because we're communicating.

You've experienced the beauty in the world, so your views are different than mine,

so maybe one day I'll learn how to properly communicate my past soul ties.

People are like light bulbs;

everyone is different and shines bright in their own way.

They also eventually go out, you never know when,

but every light has its day when it's time to go out.

Social approval is just another way of saying "I don't know myself,"

so let us ask and compare to everyone around me.

If I don't fit in, I MUST!

Standing out is frowned upon.

-Social construct

I think in my head a lot, because if I said what came to mind no one would understand.

Even I don't get it half of the time.

It's hard to explain yourself when you're still getting to know yourself.

Everyone has a story to tell how will you tell yours?

Hear my heart pounding through my chest…

I ask myself what is that?

And the world responds…

Anxiety just visiting you for the fifth time today…

-Anxiety

2014 you pushed me out on a limb.

2015 you pushed all of these new random people into my life.

2016 you presented me with a platter of betrayal.

2017 you broke my heart in more ways than one.

2018 you said you're not done learning yet.

2019… now you're ready

-College

It's okay to cry, it's okay to open up, it's okay to be vulnerable,

it's okay to be weak and open up to others who want to help.

Let it all out, it will be okay eventually, because you're not alone even though you feel like you are.

God is right there and always will be.

And here you are LIVING, despite it all!

Not sure if I miss you,

or the memories made with you.

-The one that had to go

This year was one I would've never predicted.

From the lessons to the heartache,

to the pain, to the growth,

it was definitely a year I needed to experience.

No more writing when sad

there is too much to be happy and thankful for.

Everyday proves to be a blessing,

so every day I will continue to work hard.

I lost friends, loved ones, and even myself.

At the end of it all I found God,

I found myself,

I gained family

and a new profound sense of peace.

Today I want to be quiet,

today I want to be alone,

today I don't want to do anything.

Nothing is wrong...

but today I choose me.

-Selfish

You're a FLOWER,

everyone else is a bee that wants to take from you to benefit themselves.

You produce what they want yet can't do themselves.

-Outsiders

Smiling and being happy

at the sight of rain because

the world feels how you've felt for months.

-Mirror

NOTHING makes sense,

everything else in the world is free to do

and grow and travel as they please,

except humans.

The wind blows so freely why can't that be me?

- **Nature's Freedom**

Like a tree I am planting my roots,

strengthening them, and growing strong

and tall to withstand every season.

-Growth

I write the best at night, when everyone is sleep, in the dark, my mind races.

Deep reflections at midnight, who's idea is it to keep me up?

So many things I want to say, but none of it sounds right.

I write best at night, that's when it all makes sense.

Where I was, where I am, and where I'm going.

My pain may not have been as bad as yours, but none the less it still hurts.

I write best at night; the words find me I don't find the words.

There's beauty in the silence.

The universe lets me know, you're a writer by nature, it's time to nurture the soul.

Every vein flowing through your body,

made already knowing its purpose,

must be nice knowing what you're

destined to do.

Releasing control makes you feel like you're spiraling out of control.

Why is it so hard to let something go that I never knew I had until my adult age.

To gain control you have to release it.

Be Better.

Do Better.

While everything around me falls and fails I finally feel like I'm coming to life.

From family, to friends, to the world as we knew it, it's all crumbling and appears to be chaotic.

But in the chaos, there's stillness, silent in the center of it all,

glowing brighter and brighter everyday as the chaos burns and melts away.

That stillness, that bright glowing light

is the peace in the center of me

that rises up everyday with gratitude

ready to fight the great fight.

-Living

I'm not your ordinary and let me tell you it's gotten me far.

I have a good job and I get to whip my car.

If I was just like you I wouldn't stand out, and I'm the voice of tomorrow and we ready to shout.

I'm not your ordinary, I'm going to reflect that on you.

Read that backwards it say ordinary your not,

and I believe that to be true.

Your words are your weapon, mine are my hands,

but you'll probably do more damage than I could in a lifetime.

Your words pack heat, sharp as a needle,

you don't see the pain you're causing when you blowing that steam off.

My words can sting like a bee, or sound as good as the melodies you hear walking down the street.

Did I hurt you? Did I make you feel good?

I sometimes don't know my strength when I'm filled with boiling blood.

So I'm sorry, let me start taking accountability, because the one thing I'd hate to hear is how you really feel about me.

-Accountability

Life throws me nouns as obstacles, and I respond with a verb because standing still is not an option.

You tried to distract me from my goals, turns out your "love" was all a part of the role.

You held me down so you could hold me back.

Every day with a smile then eventually you turn and laugh.

My pain is not for your entertainment I wear it on my sleeve.

I needed you more than you needed me and you knew it.

I stood up and walked away that was the resolution,

you're no longer an obstacle turns out it was all an illusion...

You hear a song; I hear my life. I hear lyrical melodies because I've had to put up a fight.

I hear the pain, sorrow, happiness, joy, all of the things I've felt.

I hear a beat that reminds me of my heart that once used to beat with the sound of love.

I hear the troubles of yesterday, the hope for tomorrow,

and the faith that helps me along the way.

I hear who I was talking to who I am, a dialogue you can't forget.

I hear my childhood in the background whispering they're proud of me.

I hear a song I can no longer sing, that person isn't me...

-Music

There's no instruction manual for life on how to handle certain situations.

You learn as you go and hopefully one day get it right.

It's not easy, and easy is boring.

The game of life, everyone forced to play, not many know how.

Laying down staring at the ceiling

wondering why me?!?!

Not knowing the potential God saw in me.

-Potential

Like the waves of the ocean,

we flow through every day of life.

Some journeys easier than others,

but all with a final destination.

Teach me how to put myself first.
Teach me how to say No.

Teach me not to feel bad.
Teach me to not feel selfish.

Teach me to be happy with doing what's best for me.

Teach me as I'm eager to learn to break the walls meant to keep me trapped.

Teach me to release the need for control.
Teach me to look toward my creator and ancestors.

Teach me to love without thought, while setting boundaries.

Teach me to align within, up, and out.
Teach me to break the barriers put up against me.

Teach me to forgive.
Teach me to keep the peace when faced with adversity.

Teach me to stay focused, grounded and disciplined.

Teach me to let go of the physicality's of life.
Teach me to answer all the questions and concerns internally.

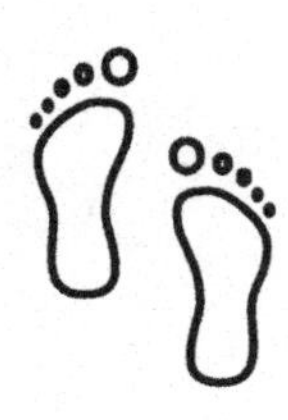

Teach me to walk in my purpose and passion.

Teach me to let go of this 9-5 and gain abundance from my passion and purpose.

Teach me to release earthly expectations.
Teach me to let go and love.

Teach me to look deeper and perform through research.

Teach me to say 'No' and be okay with it.
Teach me to communicate with my ancestors.

Teach me to understand and love the world around me.

Teach me to become one with nature.
Teach me to let go of earthly technology and thoughts.

Teach me to let go of this artificial way of living.

Teach me to appreciate life in its entirety.

I was a product of my environment.

The yelling, arguing, distrust, the faking,

there's never a solution.

When I get mad I'm furious...

even over the smallest things.

I was conditioned...

Conditioned to be selfless. But what is "self-less?"

Is it saying yes and never no?

Is it considering everyone else regardless of what's best for you?

I've been conditioned.

I am everything they said I wouldn't be,

you can't silence someone

whose actions are louder than

their words.

-Volume

I was brought up to remain silent and follow suit,

head down and do as you're told to do. Don't ask questions could be considered talking back.

And don't dare speak up against us or tell us how you truly feel, then you're disrespectful.

I was raised to be a silent mouse, to follow the rules and set a good example.

As I was told I did until I was a legal adult and not a kid.

I can't stay silent! I won't do as you please.

You can't make me feel bad for being the real me.

I've been given a voice to speak but you refuse to hear.

But I know for a fact my words will encourage people just like me far and near.

The voice I've been given is through the words I write.

-Silenced no more

Made in the USA
Columbia, SC
07 July 2023

20133188R00046